Epidemic of Nostalgia

poems by

Sujash Purna

Finishing Line Press
Georgetown, Kentucky

Epidemic of Nostalgia

Copyright © 2021 by Sujash Purna
ISBN 978-1-64662-551-2 First Edition
All rights reserved under International and Pan-American Copyright Conventions. No part of this book may be reproduced in any manner whatsoever without written permission from the publisher, except in the case of brief quotations embodied in critical articles and reviews.

ACKNOWLEDGMENTS

I am grateful for the following literary publications where these poems have appeared in earlier forms:

Gyroscope Review - Knitting
Inwood Indiana - A Sparrow
Peeking Cat Poetry - Kites on Clouds
Prachya Review - Harrowing Tale of a Tale Harrower
Prairie Winds - A Talk with the Poet
Harbinger Asylum - Sodium Vapored Growing Old
Paragon Journal - Moments and Lapses
Emrys Journal - E Pluribus Unum
Red Earth Review - Temple Juniper
34th Parallel Magazine - News from Kirksville
West Trade Review - Epidemic of Nostalgia, Energized Waters
Rigorous Magazine - The Awakening, Poached Eggs
Telepoem Booth - Lipstick Stains Poem

I am thankful to Leah Maines, the Director of Finishing Line Press, and everyone involved in the press and its diverse publications.

Publisher: Leah Huete de Maines
Editor: Christen Kincaid
Cover Art: Bishwajite Karmakar
Author Photo: Ariana Hetland-Purna
Cover Design: Elizabeth Maines McCleavy

Order online: www.finishinglinepress.com
also available on amazon.com

Author inquiries and mail orders:
Finishing Line Press
PO Box 1626
Georgetown, Kentucky 40324
USA

Table of Contents

Knitting 1

A Sparrow 2

Kites on Clouds 3

A Talk with the Poet 4

Sodium Vapored Growing Old 5

Moments and Lapses 6

E Pluribus Unum 7

Temple Juniper 8

News from Kirksville 9

Epidemic of Nostalgia 10

Remember the Fire 11

One Earth Away 13

A Sister from Bangladesh 14

The Night You Took Adderall with Wine 15

Harrowing Tale of a Tale Harrower 16

Energized Waters 17

A Christmas Gift 18

The Awakening 19

Poached Eggs 20

Lipstick Stains Poem 22

Dedicated to the wildlife that died from the bushfires in Australia

Knitting

The process is looping in and out of the tumbling blocks,
soft shadow fortes separated at the edges
measuring the dilemma, oust the threadbare,
break the ricochet: crispy thuds, a click by the napping
flesh of finger tips, a magic creating a magic,
story book, kids come and see our age old tradition
spinning out of control and making you mittens.
When it's cold outside, and not just hot chocolate,
a foam topped mousse, the off guard spill, stain
the rug and watch an avenged grief little by little
flower with spools of waves, but pools of swings.
Enrage the calm with a soothing yank,
raise a level of skirmish between the seams,
a trick or treat. Press until warm.

A Sparrow

The unflinching attitude to negativity is what keeps us alive
adored, adorned, adopted, adapted
smell of dried and burned grass and garlic
seeping through all our pedagogic minds.

When a pair of blue eyes open up
and the smell of a faint body lotion on her skin
screaming on the top of her lungs with pleasure or pain,
God knows what.

Stands out, stands in, stands better, stranded
elephant man is as beautiful as her tattoo of a sparrow
but confused as life is
a symbol just to show that we love breathing

without knowing that we do
she pulls out her notebook with non-glare white paper
with glaring dark ink and reads out;
eyes closed I listen and try hard to imagine

A black diary thrown in a trash,
a line that divides two people
inside against outside, outsider looking in,
insider looking out

at a sparrow.

Kites on Clouds

They were floating gently upon the bridge,
the breeze, breathing almost like live animals
only they were caricatures on colors, tied
to a shop of kites where I bought that t-shirt

for you, packed neatly in a paper bag when
I was walking on the boardwalk holding on to you
like I was holding on to those kites that
had sailed already, floating, breathing.

There were rare signs of surprise in their eyes;
their limbs made by men, they were on their own.
They suddenly realized they could go their own ways.
I was a fool to myself to not know then you could too

upon clouds, I could almost see you one last time,
before you melted like the distant floating kite
out of sight into the unknown,
your torn string in my palm and the t-shirt.

A Talk with the Poet

I remember an old dialogue between the poet and me
beside a grand piano.
It had reflections of the December trees
on the body of a black mahogany or oak, I can't
remember, but heard a trapped tree
calling on the wild ones outside the window.

What you can do is give more details:
what does the tea-cup look like to you?
Is it chipped? Cracked? With lipstick on it?

Details could be grains of rice submerged,
in the stolen pot heating on a time machine for food;
how great we don't have to wait anymore,
but how little we give attention to the minutiae!

Over the years will you be mine?
Or is it going to be another okay-ish shot at the image:
pigments, points, lines, and circles,
and then there is you;
smiling at me, telling me.
That's enough for today!
Let's wait a year or two?

Sodium Vapored Growing Old

Greenish beige rows of memory cartridges
with red shelves of the unwanted Tonight
could be hidden in one of those,
in its sodium vapor lamps
washing the streets and the grassy quads.

The stranger looks around for fireflies,
but none deludes him more
than those street lamps.
They have seen lives passing by,
"Some getting by and some getting old"

I thought I saw
Nick Drake walking down the corner,
taking a left turn and gone.

In a memory cartridge while in a song,
he still seems so much in the present,
except for the stranger, who is unsure?
Of what will come and what will go?
Of what will die and what will just grow old?

The serenity is in knowing that nothing is gold,
Even when the sodium vapor lamps shower
unblinkingly, we're all strangers
walking down the same streets of dreams timeless
almost like guardians of the night
and dust-filled cartridges of memories.

Moments and Lapses

My empty dorm room probably smells as same
as it did the day I arrived with my two maroon suitcases.
There was this big buzzing noise from the a/c
that rang in my ears like the plane engines of a 17-hour flight.

The empty dorm room three stories above
probably smells just the way it did when I followed her,
like a child, her hand holding mine, taking me up
to her bed, teaching me how to unhook her bra,

as we mixed Jack Daniels with Sprite, I pretended
I liked her favorite show, to show I liked her too.
The purple pillow probably smells the way
like it did the night we spent in that moon-lit room.

Four stories below those carpets on my way in
and back from work are only there to take me back
to the same smell I had to leave behind, a year ago
with two maroon suitcases and nothing else.

I remember moments and lapses, and ghosts buzzing
like bees on a honeycomb of gilded space and time.
An untrained astronaut right before the landing,
I look for the same spot, at a different time.

E Pluribus Unum

A house with two people in the summer—
heatwaves from 90s keep them from roasting.
None of the doors locks, and yet you can't
go in any of the rooms, because they are moving
in and out and away, making room for more.
The blackbird plays with the dirt in the backyard.
Wonders why a yellow volleyball net is still there
as if to scare him away any moment with newer
faces, but they show up late like a flock of tourists,
They question: How old is the house?

The stretching rabbit knows but doesn't
tell anybody from the ankle-length high plants
looks up at the black and gold plate on the wall
by the front door it reads: *e pluribus unum*
out of many, an old man in camo pants
and a glaring yellow construction cap
scares away the hundreds of years
with one flick of his thumb settling
in a new story-board the bundles gathered
and plaqu-ed a handful of asphalt
a flash of hose, diameter by diameter.

When they arrive in fall another ring
appears like Saturn's disk.
The house keeps growing older
out of many, e pluribus unum.

Temple Juniper

Outstretched and sandaled
brown feet push on the chipping away banister
like the spiderweb the memory of a quaint evening

hangs in the mind
a family of three buzzed with an American dream
by the juniper tree lay out their plans,
how to call this land their home someday

how much time and money to flow
between the time the juniper grows
in the camera and the time it's another thing
that doesn't die in the winter.

They wait until the orb of the street light
resembles the moon and the juniper cradles
into view dimly lit by a decade old lightbulb

They swing some more and then walk back home,
done with their duty: replenishing the platter,
respect to a temple of time spent by the side
an American dream, an evergreen tree.

News from Kirksville

Earlier there was a daydreaming that marched
with her kids in winter jackets looking at the big
gingerbread house inside the coffee-shop.
There was a babe in the manger. He had a language
of cries and smiles and silence, but now the kids

were not the wise-men but the giggling critics
of a late afternoon study session when you held my hand,
with your hot chocolate mocha, and I remembered
times floating past like fairies of light on a day,
before the sunset and the snow and the wind.

Did you know that
we'll be blasted off with 3 inches of snow this year?
The clasp of time holding two four-digit calendar marks,
we paint time with languages, not numbers,
they are serious work of art you don't see in the galleries,
but in your planner and in the local newspaper

that did a story on the fire that burned down;
Kirksville City Arts Center, red bricks baring souls
in charcoals, and languages that were once found
in the paintings, that are now lost in the ashes.

Epidemic of Nostalgia

On the back of a number is a song sung
in grey pencils, flying charcoal dusts
when pressed hard, it's Gatorade blue, is your
canvas of watercolors, a face popping out
like a house seen on a snowy night from a distant street
seems a home you probably wish you lived
a long ago.

What is a déjà vu if not nostalgia?
It's a phone call scene in a movie about a man
looking for love in a city full of green doors.
It's your last Christmas happening again,
when we tossed pillows in our beds
to see who grabs the bedside clock first, and
rewinds one hour, or two hours, or a day.
We knew life was going to be short;
a blink of the eye takes up one bite
of time out of it, out of yours, out of ours.
We became out of hours.

Cover yourself with a water-proof hoodie,
because I heard the snow outside tells secrets
these days, when time is too short.
It's a cliff-hanger from a TV show.
It's a heartbeat that holds your hands.
It's almost as if it's not snow, but
these seconds of our lives raining outside
at night, when everything's asleep
in the epidemic of nostalgia.

Remember the Fire

Spiritual ritual drama filling me
with agnostic view, people old and new
understand that it's okay
when they shovel the driveway
the winter back into the garage
before rooting out the budding flowers
back to concrete like they go to bed
at night, they close the blinds
in this town only you and I are safe,
rest of these creatures resist a flight
up the staircase, a banister to overlook
to see how big the living room is.

When I was 14, I picked up my first guitar
a yellow mahogany, a fake brand,
Weird Fishes Arpeggi kept ringing
as I bled my fingers across the steel
at night. Our neighbors thought:
there was a ghost living in this building
who loved to play Myxomatosis,
grilled balconies boomed with
charcoal Logitech speakers
they don't know the language,
but they could tell it was weird.
Why did I make sure my neighbors
didn't miss out? Why not now?
Annoying as the sparkler that set fire
to the hyacinths on a quaint
Diwali night, we were all busy
taking photos of men with buckets
pouring water like chords falling
down the guitar tab, with ringing splash
mixing in with the hungry ember,

the silence bursting from within,
with the resonant sound, and a fire
exploding in sparks of the subdued.
Sometimes the cold breaks the flame;
like icebergs melting in lava,
a calm night breaks into silence.

One Earth Away

Grandfathers are not hands of clocks
making sure it's our time
to come out of their sons' wives' wombs.
I lay in an armchair on a dark December night
hoping to see your ghost, but all I saw was stars
smiling like you would, if you were there.

My dad tells me you died.
No medicine. Nobody to cover your eyes.
You rose from the dead
every monsoon below the mango tree
within your broken brick kingdom,
an emperor ruled the happiest ancestors
come rain or shine.
You waited for us to know
nothing is everlasting
like the last *seuli*, night jasmines,
we all lose our fragrance and become
one body with the earth.

My dad tells me today
was your death anniversary
and how happy you'd have been
if you knew what I've been up to,
but you know you and I are
the same body, just one earth away.

A Sister from Bangladesh

a light that flickers at the end of the tunnel,
a cliché that molded you and me, we were born,
from the same mother. You are a mother now
and I am a brother that never knew you'd be one.

I ran away, got catapulted me into a world
you always wanted to go with your newly learned words.
I have become you, and you became trapped behind the window,
the room with your first kid and a spellbinding of a home

that never showed you any better, kept you like pollen
on flowers, that never left with the wind.
You were never born out of the mouth of a piano slip,
a bee-keeper's dreams to let them fly away one day.

You were captured by the man with the post and the green.
You are a beloved daughter, beloved sister, beloved mother,
beloved captured, in the shape of a bed, bringing another.

The Night You Took Adderall with Wine

Young and lost in a muddle,
a group huddled in the middle of summer heat,
body odors around the black dresses.
Black lipstick and mascara,
you came in through the dizzy lights
as I climbed up on the roof
to an Adele song and promised not
to lose you in the middle of all these
socializations that meant nothing
the next day when we'd be all sober.
Adele's cry came out the boom box
when I fought with a red-capped guy
over a long won war with my punch
drunk mind. You came close
again against my skin, an ap-
-lomb in you, a firefly that smelt
like summer on a rainy night.
On Adderall you saw me
pacing around the edge,
starchasing rooftop of a house
ground in gravity we could never
escape. We knew we were just
swinging in the summer wind.

Later that night when they all went to bed,
I found you staring into a void,
your arms shaking, Orion's bow
strung tight, you caved.
I saw a galaxy of silver stars
explode out your mouth
and into that night's sky
and never come back again.

Harrowing Tale of a Tale Harrower

Breaking clods of stories,
architecting blueprints of the amorphous,
dream shaped capsules
plopping down like pills
in beer bottles.

I am engaged in the blue-eyed barrier,
red cells collapsing in my blood shots,
hauntingly the shades of presence,
the shadows of departure
envelope the pottery,
mud-mixing make-believers-
telling tell-tale tales.

Energized Waters

I like the metallic noise that comes as a gift
with the noise of acoustic guitars. They resemble
clouds that crowd around the raining clouds,
see the shindig, have their fun, and leave.

We'll have torpor of characteristics' collisions;
positive and negative charge
giving light when they clash,
how can you gather molecules without the expertise
of a god or a higher power,
who might not even enjoy the rain?

I have seen you save a bird from dying,
a cat from drowning.
You've done more than god,
but you chose to look at the cloud wall
before a tornado, with your dad
and chose to wonder who
came before the one before the one
before the one before the one
before you.

I cannot go that far, but
did you know your great-grandfather probably
used a washboard instead of a Gibson guitar
when he wooed his wife?
He's done more than a god could.

They smiled, energized the water
molecules to form clouds
and then it rained.
You landed on earth
after a heavy downpour.

A Christmas Gift

I almost forced you to come to my memory
as if on a Ouija board, seeking a spirit. You came.
You were waiting outside the glass door
with letters from a world I have never been before.
I got distracted, a lavender smell of your hair,
I saw you standing outside, in your grey beanie-
trying to keep them from a fall to your neck;
city lights glint and lure from neon signs.
The night skyline of a city we knew so little about almost made you
its empress, maybe just for the night, or maybe it took you away from me,
just then maybe, or just until dawn came to both of us.
We were inside a glass box of a shop by the monastery;
a drizzly drowsy man in a burnt orange wrap around his body
gave me a vacant look, as I paid him and snuck a mini Buddha
in the newspaper bag, hoping not to get caught by you.
You knew, waiting outside, I got it for you for Christmas,
and I knew that by the time Buddha came out of his wrapping,
you'd be leaving a long chemtrail on a December night sky.
No longer the crown holder of this night, you would be
thousands of miles apart, from this town, from this country.
from me.

The Awakening

A hammer and sickle sticker on her lap,
the typing pad aglow in the reckoning,
hours slipped by, as the cursor moved
from blank lines to bouts of rummages
through the memory lane, and you can almost
hear the screams from the café at 9,
right before the rains start pouring outside
her words and water mixed
mud-wrestling demons released in the incubation of soul,
her arms wringing by the stack loads of hardcovers
inundating the room with her faint scent, she types on
until she reaches to the last page: references,
listing all her predecessors like recipe ingredients
for a dish made of social democracy,
for an antidote against hypocrisy.

It's 9 in the evening. The café is soon closing.
The empty armchair still exudes of her awakening,
as if Chopin into the sea,
her love for a better world
in the sands of time.

Poached Eggs

Poaching eggs with the state of the art
is a fun thing to think about,
when you think about food.

Eggs are a dream come true once
you get to live in the United States.
Save your money on groceries.

Save your time for cooking,
because you're on your own.
No bua housemaid, no sickeningly zesty

air of roasted cumin in the kitchen.
I just became a sophomore that summer
when Karly was in the laundry room-

her dad's eyes on Obama on the TV-
her mom microwaved leftovers
in red jetlagged Tupperware. Red-eyed

she said to me:
Freedom is being able to
poaching an egg
when you're hungry
in this country.

The lush white flesh
steaming over the moon
surface in wispy wafts.

A sleepy ball of yolk rolls
into your tongue,
and a sun bursts into the sky
inside your mouth.
in the USA
soft heavens on earth
not boiled, not fried,
between cooked and uncooked.
Nothing is better than this.

Lipstick Stains Poem

Your shirt with seals of colors from countries unknown
and a never-before-smelt perfume that envelops it;
a sweet fortress of aura in the invisible molecules

surrounds you, adorning you constantly when I could have sworn
I can look you in those eyes forever under the ceiling we sit,
a picture of autumn blooming in the years that flew,

like the calling geese's departure and you're a spot in noise,
a distant signal with blue lights in the sky with a limit.
I like to hold you close to me as the cruel winter prepares her rule;

you're her warm contender keeping me warm.
Tea is a fortune I can only imagine in the time before the exit
to a world full of chaos you dive in, a braver diver, a diva,

I keep your hands in mine, your lipstick stains in cups stay with me,
and an echo of your mysterious words: squad, fam and lit
keeps swirling like the wind outside with leaves, in me, in the air.

Additional Acknowledgments

I am also thankful to everyone from Department of English at Missouri State University and Department of English & Linguistics and College of Education at Truman State University, and to the following people who have inspired me or gone out of their comfort zones to support me and my poetry and without whom these poems would not have been in your hands right now:

Elahi Boksho Akanda(Dadu), Dilruba Shikha(Ammu), Zohurul Islam Tuku(Bapi), Sudhnya Amrita Islam(Didi), Ariana Hetland-Purna, Lauren Hetland, Toulouse Purna, Alana & Dan Hetland, Sushaba Haque(Tubai), Fazle Shaheen Haque, Julie Nash, Jon Hetland, Jamie D'Agostino, Joe Benevento, Hena Ahmad, Jocelyn Cullity, Alex Tetlak, Paul Yoder, Barbara Price, Naomi Shihab Nye, Jeanne Harding, Brian Cary, Emily Tolipova, Codi Caton, Nishan Adhikari, Roxanne Chong, Roshan Shrestha, Lopsang Sherpa, Bishal Lama, Ankit Shrestha, Shristi Shakya, Rezwan Arefin, Sadia Afrin, Saad Sikder, Tanjebul Alam Tasnan, Rafi Nizamee, Sakhawat Hossain Saimon, Imran Khan, Monirul Islam Nabil, Sharek Hasan, Miriam Young, Stephanie & Keevin McGlumphry, Derrick Rohr the III, Kyle Sterup, Kishor Bista, Binh T. Tran, Md. Abir Hasan Niloy, Stuti Chugh, Tatsuya Akiba, Vanessa Rivera, Pooja Aryal, Dhanushka Tennakkoon, Doralisa De Agostini, Assegid Demissie, Huy Truong, Alex Mende, Adriana Maria, Stephen Furlong, Katey Stoetzel, Kate Hawkins, Kelly Margaret Meade, Maggie & Patrick Meade, Denise Jacobson Phillips, Vertigo Xi'an Xavier, Barbara Duffey, Sam Rose, Nathan Alan Schwartz, Wolfgang Görtschacher, Lori Desrosiers, Elizabeth Hellstern, Carol Carpenter, Katherine Fortenberry, William Townsend, Lasitha Yashendra Madurawala, Jenni & Keith Ehrett, Annalisa McKenna, Jena Sterrett, Etta Madden, Marcus Cafagña, Margaret Weaver, Michael Czyzniejewski, Sara Burge, Karen Craigo, Yili Shi, Lanette Cadle, Ryan Davies, Ehsan Suez, Sinjan Majumdar, Arkanil Roy, Lane Pybas, Madison Green, Amelia Fisher, Timothy Pyatt, Rex P. Ybañez, Batool Alzuabi, Beta Lear, Austin Ball, Bishwajite Karmakar, and, last but not the least, you, the reader.

Born in Dhaka, Bangladesh **Sujash Purna** has been writing for almost half a decade. In 2012, he came to the United States on a scholarship to pursue a bachelor's degree from Truman State University in Kirksville, Missouri. Now he lives with his Iowan wife and a tabby cat in Springfield. He works at Missouri State University as a graduate assistant while completing his graduate studies.

Purna has been inspired by poets such as Walt Whitman, Agha Shahid Ali, Naomi Shihab Nye, Ocean Vuong, Terrance Hayes, Jericho Brown, Vijay Seshadri, Dilruba Ahmed, Kaveh Akbar, Ada Limón, and others. His earlier inspiration has been W.B. Yeats.

Purna's poems have been published by *The South Carolina Review, decomp, Plainsongs, Kansas City Voices, West Trade Review, Red Earth Review, Naugatuck River Review, Gyroscope Review, English Journal, Emrys Journal, Stonecoast Review, Poetry Salzburg Review, Harbinger Asylum, Havik, Prairie Winds, Peeking Cat Poetry, Inwood Indiana, Off the Coast, Novus Literary,* and others. He also has works upcoming in the *Slippery Elm Journal* and *Zocalo Public Square*.

His first chapbook *Biriyani* came out from The Poet's Haven in 2018. He has recently attended West Chester University Poetry Conference, Looking Glass Rock Writers' Conference, and Open Mouth Poetry Retreat.

CPSIA information can be obtained
at www.ICGtesting.com
Printed in the USA
LVHW010808200721
693134LV00001B/72

9 781646 625512